The Artist's Rage

A Poem by Debra Rufini

Special thanks to my illustrator, Jelena Banjac, who has so beautifully sprung this story to life.

Special thanks to my proofreader, Jo Simmonds, who has punctuated this story into perfection.

Poetry Copyright © 2024 by Debra Rufini
Illustrations Copyright © 2024 by Jelena Banjac

Refuge Publications

Hardcover ISBN: 978-0-9954914-6-5

Dedicated to the Fine Artist, Jesus Christ,

who calls us all to love – not use our boxing glove!

I also dedicate this book to the many whose lives have been affected,

or whose faith has been destroyed by those who

have been the servant in this story.

"Woe to you, teachers of the law and Pharisees, you hypocrites!

You shut the door of the Kingdom of Heaven in people's faces.

You yourselves do not enter, nor will you let those enter who are trying to."

Matthew 23:13

May this book be a big thank you to the servants who have represented

The Artist well... you know who you are.

And, may it be a big lesson to those who fail to represent The Artist,

as 'the servant' in this story does... you know who you are!

The Artist, so grateful, and so recognised,
 stood, as He thanked them and their opened eyes:
"Well done, for never a doubt for a stage –
 you never believed my lead slipped on my page."

The Artist sent the honoured and privileged few,

to 'love one another, as I have loved you.'

Hopeful in His commandment, He leaned back in His chair,

assuming His flock would show kindness and care.

"Your Honour, we'll obey what You call us to do.

We'll open their eyes to things only true.

We'll take to the streets the message You teach.

We'll take to the church the message WE preach.

We'll do it for You – our love gift for Thee.

We'll do it for them, hoping they'll look to see."

The Artist's keen servants spread widely the Word,

making sure no ear had been left unheard.

"We'll tell them the truth, come please or offend.

We can talk how we like to them – God's our best friend.

Hey you, homosexuals – yes, you – holding hands.

God says you're an abomination. You are not what God planned.

Everyone look – it's Adam and Steve!

Did you see what I did there? I rhymed it with Eve."

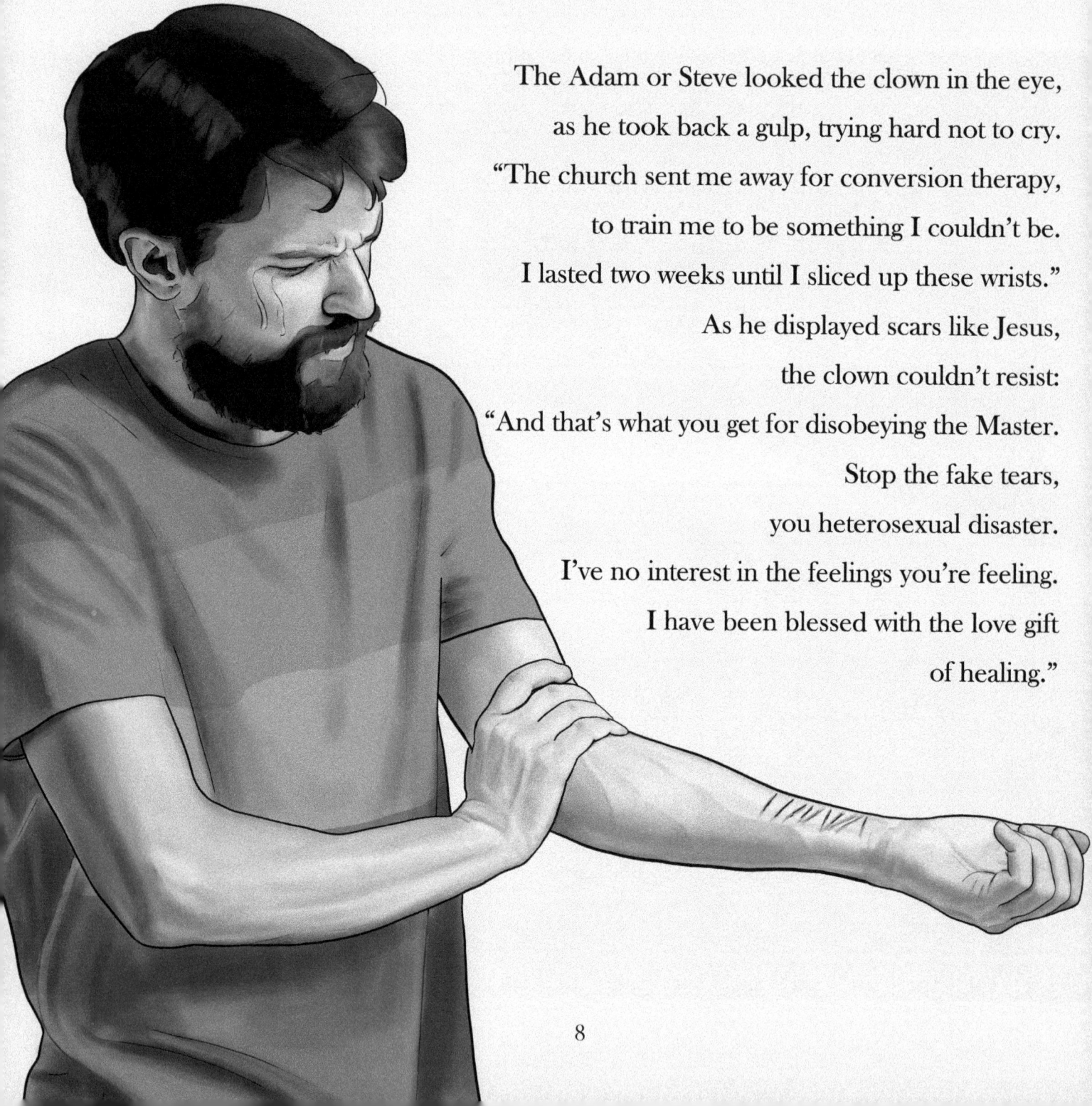

The Adam or Steve looked the clown in the eye,

as he took back a gulp, trying hard not to cry.

"The church sent me away for conversion therapy,

to train me to be something I couldn't be.

I lasted two weeks until I sliced up these wrists."

As he displayed scars like Jesus,

the clown couldn't resist:

"And that's what you get for disobeying the Master.

Stop the fake tears,

you heterosexual disaster.

I've no interest in the feelings you're feeling.

I have been blessed with the love gift

of healing."

The Artist's keen servant moved along, as he grinned:

"I'm so happy with how I've been called to honour Him.

My sandwich board's heavy, but my soul is so light.

But it is such a burden to always be right."

A mother passing by adored to hear the servant sing.

The singing servant scorned at the sight of missing wedding ring:

"Nor will the fornicators inherit the Kingdom of the Lord."

The distressed mother's baby cried at the petrifying sandwich board.

The mother gulped back tears, as she bravely began to explain:

"You have no idea, you horrid man, of my suffering and pain.

This little girl has brought me all the joy I've ever known.

I tried your God, but His PR had cast too many stones."

The mother ran off crying, as she held her baby close.

"DON'T YOU KNOW, IT'S WHORES LIKE YOU

WHO WILL INHERIT HELL THE MOST?!"

JESUS SAID: I AM THE TRUTH

14

The servant removed his sandwich board, as he prayed for all to hear:

"Thank you Lord, that I am Yours, while the others have You to fear."

An atheist had overheard the servant's boastful claim.

"What makes you certain God exists, let alone knowing His name?"

The servant proud by his reply, refused an explanation.

"All I can say is when you die, expect a confrontation."

The atheist sincerely asked how disbelief could believe.

The servant showed his sheer delight in what was up his sleeve:

"Your heart is filled with rebelliousness, where you're too blind to see.

There's no such thing as disbelief. Bow down on bended knee."

The atheist laughed the biggest laugh: "Your Jesus myth has found you."

The servant's God would not be mocked: "The evidence surrounds you."

The Master's flock approached the servant, with their joyous tear-filled eyes.

"We've won so many hearts for Him – they've come to recognise,

that The Artist's Fine Scrawl after all was never here by chance.

No pencil slipped on paper, as we all knew from the start."

Before the flock continued expressing how they'd displayed love,

the servant interrupted like an angry boxing glove:

"YOU DIDN'T JUDGE AND DAMN THEM FOR ALL ETERNITY?"

"The Master didn't tell us to – He just wanted them to see."

"I mocked two homosexuals – I called them Adam and Steve.

I made a fornicator cry, and told an atheist to believe.

It doesn't sound like you've done much, with this wishy washy love.

The Master told us to shake their vision. Take my other boxing glove."

"Don't you remember back in the studio, where we first found The Artist's gift?

We were the ones who saw it, while the others had it dismissed.

Don't you understand that some simply just don't see,

while others who have found Him have found Him differently?

The plank within our eye cannot remove their dust sized spec.

And no amount of stoning can make us sinless or perfect.

We know it's not the case at all of others adamantly not receiving.

Sometimes it's as simple as them genuinely not believing.

We cannot comprehend The Artist in His fullness now.

We cannot answer questions only He will know Himself.

We didn't come to know Him, so that we could hate those who don't.

We were called to sow Him, in the absence of those who won't."

"DON'T YOU TALK TO ME THAT WAY," said the servant in his writhing.

"I'll cause you doubt in your own faith, then blame you for your backsliding.

Your salvation is well and truly lost. The Master told me so.

My translation is the truth of Him. He told me – I should know."

The Artist was sad to see this taking place

under His nose, while ignored was His face,

as He had called them ALL to love.

"Concentrate on yourself. I'll not ask you of anyone else,

so put away your boxing glove.

I sent you to love, as I have loved you.

I called you to show kindness, and this is what you do.

What have you done in my honourable name?

You punch them, then fake me, then give them the blame.

You delight in telling my children how they're heading all for Hell.

Don't be all too certain I wouldn't send you there as well."

The Artist sank deep in His seat, as He cried:

"I never sent out servants for my love to be denied."

The Artist, so grateful when so recognised,

stands, as He thanks us when we've opened eyes.

www.ingramcontent.com/pod-product-compliance
Lightning Source LLC
Chambersburg PA
CBHW060751150426

42811CB00058B/1377